Lern Yerself Scouse

Vol. III

HOW TO TALK PROPER IN LIVERPOOL

"Yᴇ Lɪᴠᴇʀ"

BY BRIAN MINARD

Scouse Press · Liverpool

Contents

About the Author

Brian Minard was born in Liverpool in 1938. He has worked as a cab driver, an air steward, ship's writer, bacon packer, docker, barman, sales manager, carpet salesman, electro plater, roofer, has sold tinsel at Christmas and nylons at St Helens. At present he is living in New York, and since residing there has become a published poet and songwriter (he is at present under contract to Johnny Mercer for a song he wrote called "Sanctifying Grace". His travels, before going to New York, included Japan, Puerto Rico, France, New Zealand, Australia, Italy, Spain, Canada, Brazil, Egypt, Arabia, South Africa, the West Indies, Denmark, Holland, French Equatorial Africa, Malaysia, Venezuela, Portugal and China. His wife, Karen, is an ex-model and is American. They have a baby daughter, Michelle Chante.

FOREWORD

This book, unlike *Lern Yerself Scouse* (vols. 1 & 2), does not deal with the origins and sources (or, as Scouse would put it, *dtbee oranges 'n' saucers*) of Merseyside vernacular. There are two reasons for this:

a)   I have been living in New York since mid-1968, which renders any extra research or study of Liverpudlian idiom virtually impossible.

b)   I feel that nothing regarding the philology of Scouse has been overlooked by Messrs. Frank Shaw, Fritz Spiegl, Stan Kelly and Linacre Lane (*Linacre Lane?*), and therefore any further exploration would be highly impractical as well as disrespectful.

The book deals with the everyday, conversational Scousisms that add a humorous note to what could otherwise be a very drab and dun-coloured existence on and around Merseyside.

One point of interest is that, while I believe rhyming slang was not generally used by Scousers for perhaps the first half of the century, I feel that it has become prevalent over the last decade or so, quite possibly stemming from Everton's and Liverpool's football success tales, which brought thousands of fanatical Scousers in contact (often literally!) with inhabitants of other towns and cities, thus enabling the gentle Merseysiders to listen to an argot as yet unheard by them; and, as pointed out in the foreword of *Lern Yerself*

Scouse, vol. 2, 'Scouse is quite capable of appropriating any long-used word or phrase that strikes his fancy and, at a later date, swearing before God that the original user stole it from Scouse.' I have attempted to adhere to some consistent form of spelling to capture the Scouser's pronunciation, and the only point I should make is that when 'aah' or 'aahr' is seen on the following pages, it is not pronounced as in do-re-mi-fah, but is squeezed out through a tightly constricted (and possibly cartarrhal) throat — as in 'baa', the bleat of a lamb.

Useful Words and Phrases

Lenza tanner.
Could I please borrow sixpence from you?

Av gorra gerroff, am goan to ado.
I must leave, I have a party to attend.

Dthur goes 'Enree dthee eighth.
That man has a lot of children (to different women).

She billeeves in Daddy Crimbo, 'er.
She is a dullard, she is steeped in folklore.

(Crimbo = Christmas)

Ee azzin gorra potter piss in.
That gentleman's economic status leaves a lot to be desired.

Kipperonim.
He doesn't look too jolly.

Am on dthe mint.
I am employed as a dock worker.

Eez a birrova Tzony Kirtiss.
That chap is devilishly handsome.

Dzon't leave dthe buss wid a guilty conscience.
(said by a bus conductor)
I hope you have all tendered your fares.

Eez gorra banger.
That chap owns a rather old-fashioned, second-hand car.
or
That child is in possession of a very explosive firework.
or
He has a sausage on his plate, why haven't I?

Av gorra 'and like a futt.
*I am gambling, but I don't have too much confidence
in the cards that have been dealt to me.*

Eez gorraahfacrown on iz 'ead.
He has a small bald spot at the back.

Offun.
Quite regularly.

Offunnon.
From time to time.

Zarrafact?
Is that true?

Yerrokay.
If you have told me this once, you have told me a thousand times, now let us terminate this pointless discussion.

Caahn't fid dthe Bob 'Ope.
I am having difficulty in locating the soap.

Ee kin peel an orange inniz pockit.
He is rather miserly.

She caahnaahf chant.
That female is a remarkably good singer.

Owl fashioned 'eels.
Means that the person referred to is 'quite shrewd'.

Obstroculus.
The Liverpool version of 'obstreperous'.

Fine owjadoo izzinid?
This can only be described as a catastrophe!

Am Joe Palookad.
In this game of snooker you have been artful enough to place the cueball in such a position that I find it impossible to hit a red, let alone score.

(A cry of dismay often heard in the old 'Marionette' in Lime Street.)

Avyer bin X-rayed yet?
Have you received your wage packet up to now?

Firgott me saahnys.
I left my lunch at home.

(More often than not, the lunch hasn't been left at home at all; the wife or mother, whichever the case may be, has usually refused to make any sandwiches because of his or her persistent late-night gallivanting.)

Eez a bit Mutt 'n' Jeff.
He is a trifle hard of hearing.

(At one stage of the game I was employed as a 'fruit skin' and was working down at Gladstone Dock with a couple of other fellows. Our foreman or overseer was an ill-tempered, ungrateful type of individual who used to spend most of his working day sitting on a bollard, gazing into space.
He was in this position one day when an out-of-town driver came looking for him. We pointed the foreman out to him, adding that he was extremely hard of hearing and that only shouting directly into his ear would have any effect at all. The driver went over and literally screamed into his ear that he had a delivery. I don't know about HIM having a delivery, the foreman nearly had a delivery . . . of twins! When the driver turned to look for the three fellows in question, all that was visible was an empty space.)

Gyar blimee.
I am overwhelmed.

Jumpun jee hoasofat.
My goodness!

Goan ommee welt.
I am about to take my mid-morning break.

Yikkud 'ire dthem out fer gondolazzin Venice.
Your shoes are quite large, aren't they?

Al avva birra Grace Kelly aftir.
I will watch TV later on.

Am goan fer me groceries.
I am going home to eat.

Dthe bagga yeast caahn aahf rabbit.
The Reverend Father's sermon is rather lengthy.

Oozee?
I haven't seen that chap before.

Now att.
A friendly remark to anyone in Liverpool wearing headgear.

Mint imperial.
A Liverpudlian version of 'immaterial'.

Folly me leedzer.
I am directly behind you.

(A term often used by middle-aged and tipsy Liverpool housewives as they follow the lady who is holding the 'kitty' into pubs in Blackpool or Morecambe on 'Ladies' Night Out'.)

Giz a bice!
Your apple looks decidedly good.

Giv us me caardz.
I have no desire to work here any longer.

(An excellent example of how Scouse can use both plural and singular in the same sentence, to mean exactly the same thing.)

He lispeth sailor.
Richard Burton's wife.

Eez an aahrtiss.
He paints pictures for a living (often said with a look of disbelief).

An asperro.
A pain-relieving tablet.

Gotyigeet?
Have you brought your guitar?

Cumoffut!
I find that somewhat difficult to believe.

Am goan dthrew dthe pipe.
I am travelling via the Mersey Tunnel.

Eez gorra bike onniz nose.
He wears spectacles.

Rambullon.
Talk if you wish, I am paying not the slightest attention.

Goan back dthe rivierra dthis yeer.
My holiday will be spent in the Isle of Man again.

Erz aah rennery.
This is where we keep the poultry.

Sold!
This article is definitely not new.

Sod dthat!
I am not going to carry out this particular task.

Less gerra Joe Baksi.
We will ride by cab.

Am droarrun.
I am sketching.

Wirse meedickshinree?
I cannot find my lexicon.

Eez gorra fedtherrup is aahrse.
He is in a very jovial mood.

Ee leff me!   *(uttered in a tone of disbelief)*
The bus driver has failed to stop.
or
My husband has left home.

Dthe blooz lost.
Means a dreadful weekend ahead.

Dthe redz lost.
Means exactly the same.

Stirring.
Twine.

Theezur thum.
Those are they.

Aorta.
He really should.

Humps Haven.
I am putting money in the bank every week.

Dthee owsa plenty.
The local National Assistance Board.

Choir.
Please! Less noise!

Twat dthat!
That person does not rank very highly in my esteem.

Aah yer grafton?
Have you been fortunate enough to secure employment of late?

Madlad.
An exuberant, high-spirited youth (an affectionate sobriquet).

Sarawak.
Farewell, friend.

Noat awkun to um.
means that a male member of the community has attained a modicum of respectability and it is now rather difficult to communicate with him.

(The American version is: 'That guy keeps giving me a busy signal.')

Eez bin vaccinated wid a grammyphone needle.
He is very talkative.

25

Av dun me poke in on dthe gee gees.
*I have been gaming at the sport of Kings, my losses
were substantial and I am bereft of pocket money.*

(The American version is: 'I dumped a bundle at the track.')

Am on dthe Nat King.
*I am currently unemployed, I am collecting social
benefits.*

Eez a Tom Pepper, 'im.
That man tells lies very frequently.

Days of the week:
Mundee, Chewsdee, Wensdee, Thirsty, Fridee, Satdee,
Sundee.

Nowd then cod's 'ead!
Greetings, my friend.

Ee pen 'n' inks.
There is a distinct odour emanating from that chap.

Magistrate.
Marjorie can be trusted, she is wholly honest.

Erz crater face.
Here comes that person who suffers from acne.

Seven.
This is total bliss.

Or rice.
Very well then. (Usually said with a sigh of resignation.)

Doh mind **or** Wooden say no.
Thank you very much; I should like to accept your offer.

Sid Samsonite?
Do you have an appointment with Samuel this evening?

Ammonia cleaner.
I am merely a floorwasher.

Simple tin!
Oh, you ridiculous fellow!

Ister sign o' dthe cross!
Beware! It's the boss.

Deduct.
They lowered their heads.

Anbrosia dinyew.
My complexion is pinker than yours.

Jules az gone.
Precious stones are missing.

Dirronda Rocky Racoon.
The astronauts have landed upon the lunar surface.

Gabbreez nack.
A chocolate covered shortbread (Cadbury's Snack).

She caahn aahf jangle.
That woman is rather garrulous.

Zanny got dthe bullet.
Daniel was sacked.

Gowss.
A very painful swelling of the feet or joints.

Eez gorra 'ead like a rosary bead.
He keeps his hair rather closely cropped.

Yinneed a pairra bellers upyer aahrse.
You have attempted to light that cigarette three times,
to my knowledge.

Avenue.
Have you not?

Eez a case 'im.
That bloke really is amusing.

Myra's well.
Oh, I suppose I should.

Avyer bin weighed off yea?
Have they paid you what they owe you?

31

Maahrk iz caahrd.
Enlighten him.

Avyer gorra brewer wha?
Have you brought sufficient tea, sugar and milk to provide us with mid-morning refreshments?

Liverpudlianisms directed at miserly folk:
Wooden givyerra fright iffee wuz a ghost.
Erz owl scatter dthe cash.
Wooden givyerra spot iffee 'ad pimples.
Eez got moths inniz wollit.
Wooden givyerra galassa worterrin dthe desert.
Yiv got more chance o' dthe Queen buyin' yerra bevy.
Ee wooden pissonyerrif yer wuz on fire.

Eez gorriz pockits soan up.
She dozen know dthe new munny's out.

Eez a backbencher.
He isn't much of a conversationalist.

Pope's Corner.
*A part of Woolton which contains several convents and
other Roman Catholic establishments.*

Avvad me orders!
I have been invited out by an affluent chap (spoken gleefully).

Lookid the bewdle onnim!
My word! that fellow has a large nose.

Eez a birrova divvy.
He isn't too intelligent.

Gunnite.
See you tomorrow.

Dthe Sally Aahrmy.
The Salvation Army.

Inchee?
Is she not?

Sapphire ter dthis laz. *(A dockers' expression)*
Would you be kind enough to light my cigarette, sir?

Eez a lemmin pelter.
He belongs to the Loyal Order of the Orange Lodge.

Sheez tawkun in tellyphone numbers aggen.
Means that the female referred to, although of the same
environment and status as the rest of the community,
is constantly mentioning the huge, but fictitious, sums
of money that have been, are, or will be passing through
her greedy but empty hands.

Arry Carry.
A Japanese form of suicide.

Birbgum.
A city in the Midlands of England.

That's dead Andy.
This is really most convenient.

Dthee aahrth.
The fireplace.

Seaman Lee.
It would appear that . . .

Beer mannan Jack!
Stick to your principles! Damn the job!

('To Jack' means, in the building trade, to quit.)

Dthe lantern stage.
Where the Birkenhead Ferry ties up.

36

Wonna cowjooce.
A bottle of milk, please.

Dthurz jaspers 'ere.
I have noticed cockroaches on the premises.

Old Don.
Wait one moment.

Early morning dialogue in Great Crosshall Street:
*Woman in rollers, leaning idly on her second floor
window sill, says to Postman:*
Ay laz, am **w**ait'n' fer sum mail.

37

Postman:
Aah yer girl? I yope ee tirnz up.

Raah yer!
Where are you?

Some Liverpudlian derivatives of people's names

Christian names		Surnames	
Peter	Pop	*Dalton*	Dollo
Tom	Tosh	*Morris*	Moggsy
Frank	Yank	*Hughes*	Yozzer
Philip	Filly	*Murphy*	Muff
George	Judda	*Ferguson*	Fair go
Gabriel	Gabby	*Taylor*	Tayo

John	Jack	*O'Brien*	Oabee
Cyril	Squirrel	*Machonochie*	Conk
Harold	H.	*Warner*	Wogs
Laurence	Lol	*Smith*	Smigger
Joseph	Jobo	*White*	Persil
James	Jazzer	*McLaughlin*	Gloc
Marjorie	Madge	*Timpson*	Timmo
Veronica	Verra	*Kelly*	Kelloggs
Gerald	Lel	*Salmon*	Sockeye
Bernard	Barney	*Ball* (one in particular)	God

Dozen know is aahrse frum is elbow.
He is a rather inefficient type of person.

Itzaz cold azza witche's tit.
It is indeed chilly.

Goan fimmy Crimbo din-din.
I am going to partake of Christmas fare.

Am gaffless.
At present, I have nowhere to live.

('Me gaff' meaning my flat, house, etc.)

Av got mobile dandruff!!
I have body lice.

Av gottoo weeks o' boozun 'n' snoozun.
Well, my annual two week holiday is here once again.

Al see yerrin Tin Can Alley.
Let's meet at Otterspool Promenade.

Otterspool Promenade was formerly a rubbish dump which has now been landscaped and is Liverpool's equivalent of the American "Drive In" cinema. Hundreds of cars each day are driven there, especially after the hour of dusk, so that couples can admire the view over the Mersey through completely steamed-up windows.

I yad icicles ommee tool!!
The mercury was a little below forty-five degrees.

Eez got lemonjitis, 'im!
My husband is partial to a wedge of lemon with his Friday fish.

A garnished dish is, of course, unheard of in Liverpool — where I came from, anyway.

Dthe jook.
Prince Philip.

Philip an' all iz bleedn relatives.
Philip, Son & Nephew Ltd, the well-known Liverpool bookshop.

Dthe jooker Kent.
The rent.

Av loss me parrot, it wuz a tooer.
A complaint voiced by children when someone has won a red and white marble from them.

Sheez offer chump.
The lady is slightly deranged.

The body

(the more familiar, nationally used euphemisms and dysphemisms
have been excluded)

The Hair	County Kildare, Barnet, Vanity Fair
The Face	Boat Race, Kipper
The Head	Loaf of Bread, Barnet, Bonce
The Eyes	Mince Pies, Peepers
The Nose	I suppose, Bugle, Hooter
The Mouth	North and South, Gob, Cakehole
The Teeth	Hampstead Heath, Cowdenbeath, Railings
The Chin	Vera Lynn
The Ears	Flappers
The Neck	Gregory Peck
The Chest	Coat and Vest
The Breasts	Mae Wests, Manchester Cities, Shelf Kit, Milkshakes, Bristol (City)

The Belly	Paddy Kelly, Gut, Bread Basket
The Testicles	Orchestra Stalls, Niagara Falls, Jocks, Goolies, C(l)ockweights, Marbles
The Clitoris	Little Man in a Boat, Hotspot
The Legs	Dolly Pegs, Pins
The Feet	Plates of Meat, Boats, Plawts
The Hands	Elastic Bands, Forks
The Sideburns	Louse Ladders
To Urinate	Slash, Hit and Miss, Lag, Jimmy Riddle
The Faeces	Pony and Trap, Arabian Night, Eartha Kitt
The Vagina	Claptrap, Flycatcher, Penwiper (obs.), Confessional, Dripping-pan, Bellydingle, House of Commons (a prostitute's), Poor Man's Blessing, Cockholder (also used of the penis — i.e. a corruption of *cuckolder*?),

Quim (corruption of *quoniam*, used since medieval times), Crinkum-Crankum (cf. John Aubrey's *Brief Lives*), Sharp and Blunt.

Light-hearted Scousisms for the penis:
Nudger, Chopper, Tool, Mutton Dagger, Pork Sword, Weapon, One-eyed Milkman, Three for a Bob, 'Ampton (e.g. 'Never gettyer 'Ampton Court'), Ding Dong, Tadger, Buzz Bomb, Dickie Die Doe.

Clothes

Shoes	St. Louis Blues, Daisies
Gloves	Turtle Doves
Wig	Irish Jig

Make-up	Warpaint, A Face
Shirt	Dicky Dirt (hence *Dicky* for false shirtfront)
Tie	Mincer (derivative of Mince Pie)
Coat	Nanny Goat
Overcoat	Smother, Pony and Float
Trousers	Strides, Toffee Rex (rhyming with keks)
Underpants	Toffees (as above)
Panties	Ditto
Socks	Mint Rocks
Scarf	Inch and a Half
Hat	Caydee
Watch	Kettle
Ring	Groin
Spectacles	Bike, Radar Gear

Eating and Drinking

Giz aahf a bitter laz, 'm paarched.
Would you oblige me with a half-pint of your light ale,
sir, I have a burning thirst.

Gedtheeaylin!
Would you be kind enough to replenish our glasses?

A remark made, usually, by one of a company of drinkers in a public
house to another in the same company, who has probably, owing to
lapse of memory, omitted to pay his turn for alcoholic beverages.

See 'im, eez loatet.
You are looking at a very wealthy gentleman.

47

Laahj wite!
A double portion of Australian White Mountain wine, please.

A cry heard in any of Liverpool's (six?) Wine Lodges.

Ee zad one over dthee eight.
*In Liverpool, means that the person referred to has had at **least** thirteen pints of beer.*

A minesweeper.
A person who steals drinks from the bar or table when the owners of the drinks are not looking.

Eez awright, eez merry.
Don't pay too much attention to him, he is senseless with drink.

Gizzasiggy.
Would you be kind enough to give me a cigarette?

Am baylun out, am bevvied.
I must depart, I have consumed too much alcohol.

Eh laz, wurz dthe bog?
Excuse me, sir, would you direct me to the toilet?

It's a friggin' sin!
Somebody has dropped and broken a bottle of beer.

Yer awright, it's ony a lackey dthat!
Calm yourself, he is merely the manager.

Or luk out, erz Frank Zinaahtra.
A gentleman in the pub would like to sing a song.

Fill yer boots, wer all go un ter Blackpool.
Drink heartily, old chap, plenty for everybody.

Am goan furrajill.
Don't wait up for me, I intend to get drunk.

Al be in dthe chinx.
I can be located at the Chinese restaurant.

'Ullo? Fire deepaahrtmint? Thurz a fire in dthe nightclub.
I have just been refused admission to the nightclub!

Rockefelluzin.
The gentleman who purchases but one glass of beer each evening has arrived at the bar.

Put yerrandin yer pockit!
Come along, you skinflint! Buy a drink.

Zing! Yew!
How about giving us a song?

Shurrup annavva bevy.
Talk a little less and drink a little more.

Used a lot by husbands to wives.

A wonna livener.
I drank a lot last night, but I must slake my thirst yet again this morning.

Short pub conversation:

Customer: Avyer seen Phyllis?
Barman: Phyllis oo?
Customer: Phyllis bleedin' glass up.

A plater jockeys.
A portion of French Fried potatoes.

A see all dthe clergy's 'ere.
I notice that most of the vagabonds, thieves, rogues and burglars are present.

Regularly heard in Liverpool homes on Saturday afternoons, after the pubs are closed.

Grid downya.
Drink it, it's only your twelfth pint of beer.

This lumberron dthee olla.
There is a brawl on the waste ground.

Ponta jungul jooce!
I'll try a pint of your best bitter, sir.

Well-known Liverpool public house conversation:
Wot wujja like luv?
Gin 'n' orange.
Two aahves a bitter pal.

Avva dropper lotion.
Come, imbibe!

Cuppa tea anna wuddy. (Woodbine)
The Scouse definition of breakfast.

Chairs.
Good Health!

Bollasass.
One container of your Sarsaparilla, please.

Lasted ur big tzime spenders.
A waitress's disgusted reaction to the sixpence gratuity she has just received from a Scouse customer.

Dthat feller spills Maud nigh drink.
That chap has an amazing capacity for alcohol.

Dthrow us the Calcutta.
Please pass the margarine.

Oo! Luk wha' dthe gud furry leff me!
*I was artful enough to hide a bottle of beer earlier in
the evening. This is it! Cheers!*

Schew.
Another name for the Liverpool dish, Scouse.

Eez chemicked!
He is inebriated.

Crime and Punishment

Kekka mush dtherz a musker ind thee 'aystack.
*Say no more, my friend, there happens to be a
policeman behind you and he may be eavesdropping.*

Dzerez a Jam Bhutty Car!
Here is a police patrol car.

Jam butty = jam sandwich. The name is derived from the
horizontal red stripe (the filling!) painted on some police cars.

Dthe jaxorrear!
The detectives have arrived!

Saychoyss.
Enough conversation, my man, the walls have ears.

Dthe scuffers nicked 'im.
The police apprehended him.

A loader Tom went off lass nite.
A number of gems were stolen last night.
(Underworld cant.)

Knit!
Be quiet and sew your mailbag.

Tzony gorra caahrpet.
Antony was sentenced to three months imprisonment.

Ease out.
My husband (or son) is not at home.

Policemen and warrant officers hear this phrase with monotonous regularity.

De Ville.
Pentonville Prison.

Gommee collar felt.
I was charged with committing a felony.

Nabisco.
Steal his jacket.

Fell offer backuva lorry.
Here is a real bargain!

Gorridin Paddy's Maahrkit.
*The standard Scouse reply when asked the origin of an
expensive article, such as a Jaguar car, a solid gold watch,
a diamond ring, etc.*

Eez doon a birra porrij.
He is serving a prison sentence.

Love and Courtship

Dijja givver won?
Did you have sexual relations with that young lady?

Lookid dthee aahrse on dthat!
*Have you noticed the anatomical distribution of that
female's behind?*

Tirraah, siettumorra.
*Not — incredibly — Gaelic, but a parting phrase used
by young Liverpool lovers as they bid each other
farewell for the evening.*

Duz she do a tirn?
Does that maiden believe in free love?

When a young man is attempting to establish rapport with a comely female, he is often given encouragement from his friends with whispers of:

Stick yer 'and upper frock.
Buy 'er a pint.
Asker 'as she got folse teeth.
She's like a docker wit lipstick.
She's gorra mustache.
Asker 'ow much she chaarges to 'ornt a 'ouse.
Givverra flash.
Is she in dthe commandos?
Purra sack over 'er 'ead.
Chinner!
Butter!
Givverra belt!

Kicker!
She's not bad ferra bulldzog.
Av seen berra faces on clocks.
Asker 'as she gorrany cash.
She's a brass.
She juss faahted.
She luks like Churchill.
Thrower a bone.
Wot number bus 'it 'er?
She kin eat a banaahna sideways.
Chaser!
It's a fella deressed up.

Get yer keks off luv.
Please remove your panties, my dear.

61

She's gorra face like an ole manz knee.
Her physiognomy could not be described as classic.

A Fancier.
*I **am** attracted to that damsel.*

She's dthe villige bike.
She is known to be rather liberal with her amorous favours.

The American version is: 'She's a gangbang'.

Gerrab me mitt.
Come, take my hand.

Awright girl?
Good day, madam or *Did you experience an orgasm?*

She's abou' seven futt tall.
The lady is a little over five foot eight.

Av seen more meat inna priest's 'ouse onna Gud Fridee.
He or she is rather slender.

Givuzz a Tate 'n' Lyle.
Come, come, now, how about a grin?

Tored the toffees offer.
I had sexual intercourse with that woman.

She's wearrun crap gear.
That young lady is hardly the epitome of sartorial elegance.

She kin eatan apple dthrough a tennis rackit.
She has slightly prominent teeth.

Norrunutha won!!
Are you really pregnant again, darling?

Sheez a birrova crank.
That woman has a very tart disposition.

Sheik'n sing a jewett onner own.
That lass is rather plump.

Dthurz Gypsy Rosalee.
Indicates that a woman with Latin features is in the immediate surroundings.

Copferracracker lass nite.
I met a delightful member of the opposite sex yesterday evening.

She's gorra pursnality like a nopen grave.
She is a rather dreary girl, she will have difficulty in finding a husband.

Eez bin knocked back *(turned down)* by so menny birdz, ee shud be in dthe Ginniss bewkarecords.
A familiar Liverpool phrase regarding an unfortunate, would-be Casanova.

Dijja gerra blimp?
Did you manage to peek up that girl's skirt?

I believe blimp came from Colonel Blimp, a film about a soldier who was constantly adjusting his monocle to achieve a better view of things. Possibly, I'm not sure.

That wons like a bleedin' 'orse.
She is not too attractive.

Sheez got legs like knotty pine.
She has grotesque legs.

Genoa?
Do you know who that lady is?

Eez a shirtlifter.
He is attracted to members of his own sex.

A drroppdum.
I took down my panties.

Gerragerrippovver.
After the damsel, lad! He who hesitates is lost.

Assert.
A woman who cannot say 'no' to amorous advances.

Slike a mop 'angin' over dthe bannisters.
Her hair is rather untidy.

Birrovva libbitty.
She got him to buy the engagement ring while he was under the influence of drink; she took rather unfair advantage.

Goan dthe jazz?
Will you accompany me to the ballroom?

Dtha birdz gorra birra class.
She puts the light off before undressing in a strange
man's room.

Adjust.
I have, recently.

I yad a cuppa tea anna blowthrough.
I slept with an unknown young lady . . . a ship that
passed in the night.

Sheez gorra naughty pin.
Her legs are not too shapely.

Erz Maahrks 'n' Spencer.
The couple approaching have been courting for twelve years.

I only gorra birra finger pie.
*I did not **quite** succeed with that girl.*
or
That chap isn't as ardent as he is made out to be.

She wuz awright ter practise on.
The regretful philosophy of a Liverpudlian who has been jilted by his lover.

Ow wujja like ter wirk under me, girl?
Not an offer of employment, but an invitation to sexual callisthenics.

Ew. A feela *shamed!*
Means that an unattractive male has just asked a young
lady, who is drinking in a Wine Lodge, if he may escort
her home. The lady's exclamation of horror is often
parried by the male with:
Yer doan dthink a meant idooya?
as he turns on his heel..

The Family and Friends

Wotch yer doan pusher eye out.
Remove your finger from your nose immediately!

Unnook!
Good Heavens! I have told you repeatedly about
picking your nose, now stop it!

70

Wirzmeemam?
Are you cognizant of the whereabouts of my mother?

A plaintive cry of children under twenty-five years of age. After
twenty-five this is usually forsaken for: 'Where *is* she?

Am gornto inspect the back o' me eyelids.
I am tired, I must take a nap.

Me yowl girl's gone dthee 'ousey.
My mother is having an evening of bingo.

Am gazumped.
I am extremely weary.

Me kettle's in dthe Mountains o' Morn.
My watch has been pledged to the pawnbroker.

A think aah kid's kweer.
*My brother is fifteen and, as yet, has not been to bed
with a female or been arrested.*

Eez a birrovva Beatle.
He plays the guitar.

Me yowl fellaz attid aggen.
*I regret to say that my father is drinking heavily once
more.*

Dthe chaveez a karracker!
That small child is very beautiful.

Aggeez on dthe bucket.
Agnes has slipped out to the toilet.

Jeeeeeziz!!!! Nertuk the friggin' 'and off meself.
Dash! I've just tapped my thumb with the hammer.

My Krise! eez fit fer nothink dthat kid!
My young son isn't too brilliant.

Ee caahn aahf nosh.
That boy has a healthy appetite.

Frankenstein's cummun ternite.
My mother-in-law is visiting us this evening.

Avyer been dthe chippy?
Is my evening meal prepared?

Por Bastud!
He has recently married.

73

Ooze apple taahrted?
I suspect somebody in the company of breaking wind.

Sheez an effin' newsince, 'er.
My sister is rather a pest.

Wotz dthat!!!
*I am not too pleased with the meal you have set
before me.*

Saytn 'imself!
*Means, usually, that the rent collector has paid a
surprise visit — probably to plead for some back rent.*

Ornoh! Norraggen!
I see my cousin coming with his seven children.

Phrases of endearment from Liverpudlian fathers and mothers to their three- and four-month-old sons and daughters:

'Ullo dthur fish face.

Woss the marrer wid me lil barrel?

Yer lil fat frog.

Gizza kiss baldy.

Dthank God yer doan luk like yer granmah.

A no wot yor do un.

Gib'm a derrop o' Ginniss, no aahrm.

A dthink al put yerrin a butty.

Wonna wotch dthe telly?

Pull dthe dzoggy's tail.

Oo, me knees all warm.

Yer biggerd'n 'im nex dor.

Dthass noverry lady like.
Doan cry queen, yer nanny's goan soon.
Yer luk mor like me'd'n 'er. *(whispered)*
Doan put me sock in yer moudth laz.
Dthur trine a pin sumthink on yew.
We corled yerrafter 'er so's she might givvus a few bob.
Ay Ay, av juss changed yer.
Cummon dthen, avva lil kipwack.
Worra grotty ole botty.
Wish yer cud tork.
Sheez got dimpills inerrands!
Eat yer milk, girl.
Gobblesser, sheez gorra voice like a bosin.
Now dthen chubby, owz yer belly offer spots?
Sheez blowun dthim out dthe back aggen.

Muss bee Satdee nite.
The lady next door is not wearing rollers in her hair.

Very nice izzunid?
She is pregnant and not yet married.

Larry Olivier.
Laurence, this is my home.

Crackerjack!
Chastise her, John.

Am wearyfied.
I am very sleepy.

Sired, goan Tibet.
I have had an exhausting day . . . time for my nightly rest.

Am bacon dthis avvy.
I will be cooking bread and cakes this afternoon.

Avyerrad yerrangry pill?
You are not in a very agreeable mood.

Wotcha doan birn yerration bewk!
*Said by a husband to his spouse when the wife (who is
known to be unfaithful by all and sundry) is sitting on
a chair in front of the fire, with her feet on the mantlepiece!*

Lookow! Catch it.
Step warily, a feline quadruped has soiled the linoleum.

And see May.
Aunt Mary.

Take id easy sun. Thiz two prizez!
Don't eat so quickly, my boy.

The Studied Insult

Fir coat an' no drawers.
*A derogatory phrase generally implying that although a
certain lady in the immediate vicinity may be sporting
a diamond ring, or is perhaps planning a holiday in
Spain, she is not a very good housekeeper and has
been known to fall behind with her rent on occasions.*

Be livvun in Formby nex.
*The person referred to has had rather rapid promotion,
entailing financial elevation, and could possibly leave
the neighbourhood for better surroundings.*

Ooer yew?
*I am of the same intellectual, social and economic
status as yourself; why try to indoctrinate me to
your way of thinking?*

Upyer pipe!
*Very well, I have listened to you, but nonetheless I
have no respect for your admonishment.*

'Op it.
Please leave my company.

My lad stanz aloan!
*I have had a couple of Guinness, I feel I should tell
you that my son is rare and unique.*

Eh! Moudth!
*I would appreciate it if you would stop interrupting
my conversation.*

This term is usually addressed to members of the family, e.g. to a
wife or a younger brother.

Prick, dthat!
He isn't a very fine fellow at all.

Av seen more blud in a banaahna.
The person alluded to is uncommonly pale.

Jump onniz 'ead.
Ask that chap to be quiet.

Gorra birrovva gash 'n' dthee roped me up.
I sustained a cut and had stitches inserted.

Dthe jumped up, never cum down, no gud, silly born bastud.
An expression of disapproval.

Eez lost iz rag.
He is obviously annoyed.

Erz sane Joseph.
Here comes a bloke wearing a two-tone jacket.

Achindim.
*Not Hindi, but a purely Scouse expression: I hit him
a blow on the jaw.*

Aplantudum.
Not Latin — I delivered a punch to his cheek.

Eez a birrovva soap wrapper.
That chap is a pugilist.

Ittim now sun, yiv got dthe wind wijja.
*A phrase often heard at Liverpool Stadium and addressed
to the weaker of two boxers.*

At the Football Match

Eez gorra backonim like a ware'ouse rat.
My word! What a hefty fellow.

When somebody who doesn't really 'belong' tries to
impress people around him at a football match by saying:
Ooze dthe ref terday?
he is often greeted by the acid remark:
Dthe fellerin dthe black suit.

Wingers birrovva torssus.
The outside forward isn't too speedy.

Ee gets ourra breath wen ee cleans iz teedth.
The centre forward isn't as physically fit as he could be.

Moggsy deefectud.
Liverpool's outside forward signed for Everton (uttered
in a tone of incredulity).

Pelly.
An amazing footballer who plays for Santos and Brazil.

Gorn dthe mach?
Will you be attending the soccer game this afternoon?

Ee ay addio *is known as* Dthe bat lim.
The Battle Hymn.

Miscellaneous

Money (pre-decimalisation)

½d	A Meg
1d	A Clod
3d	A Joey
6d	A Sprarzy, a Tanner

1/-	A Chip
2/-	Two Og
2/6d	A Tosheroon, Half a Dollar
5/-	An Oxford Scholar
7/6d	Three Half Crowns
10/-	Cow's Calf, Half a Quid, Half a Bar
£1	A Oncer, a Plymouth Sound, a Nicker
£2	A Deuce, a Dewybar
£4	A Rofe
£5	A Handful, a Ching, a Fiver
£10	A Tenner
£20	A Score of Quids
£25	A Pony
£50	Half Hundred
£100	A Ton

| £500 | A Monkey |
| £1,000 | A Grand, a Long One |

More Useful Words

The Home

Stairs	Dancers
House	Drom, Ken, Gaff
Toilet	Carzy, Bog, Bucket, Thinking Room
Guitar	Geet
Bed	Flock, Wagon, Shitcart
Football	Casey
Dog	Mutt
Cat	Moggy
Husband	My Feller
Wife	Me Missis

Baby	Chavvy
Father	Old Feller
Mother	Old Girl
Brother	Our Kid

Sundries

Car	Screeve
Drambuie	Drum Boogie
Dancehall	Jazz
Woman/Girl	Creamy Whirl, Bird, Mannishin
Man/Boy	Mush, Geezer
Prison	Nick, Blue Brick, Joe Gerk's
Cigarettes	Snout, Burn, Siggies, Coffin Nails
Beautiful	Custy, Ream, a Cracker, Not Too Foul

Job	Graft
A Fight	A Scrap, a Lumber, a Go
Cockroach	Jasper
Homosexual	Shirtlifter, Punk, Queer, Turd Burglar
Promiscuous woman	Brass, Pallyass, Good Thing, Cert, Charva
Money	Readies, Poke, Bran Mash, Ackers
Policemen	Old Bill, Busys, Muskers, Mingees
Detectives	Jacks, Old Bill, Plainees
Jewellery	Tomfoolery, Ice
Suntan	Bronzy
Rain	Parny
Sexual intercourse	Dover, Sausage, Half Hundred, Rumpy Pumpy
Trouble	Lumber, Aggra(vation)

Food

Tea, Sugar and Milk	A Brew
Beef Stew	Scouse
Coffee	Cup of Everton (Everton Toffee)
Oysters	Depth Charges
Eggs	Hen Fruit
Peas/Beans	Wind Instruments
Caviar	Black Tapioca
Sandwich	Butty
V.D.	Half a Gross (Dose), Sore Toe
Annoyed	Got the Needle, Got the Spike
Newspaper	Linenn, Blad
Rest period	Welt, Blow

On Board Ship

Doan snap yiffingers amee. I'm no dzog!
*An exclamation hurled at the passenger who has, usually,
paid an astronomical sum to travel the high seas and who,
in all innocence, thinks that the pictures of the smiling
waiters he saw in the many pre-voyage brochures are,
in actual fact, the ones zipping around the dining saloon
with a slightly glazed look in their eyes . . . ah! the
innocence of youth.*

Avyer mustard?
Have you reported for work? (Muster=report)

Am goan firra baggoff.
I am going to pay a call on the local brothel.

91

Dthe bludz on yeah?
Have the passengers begun to embark? (Bloods=passengers)

Av gottoo eights in dthee annexe.
*I have eight passengers at each sitting, and my tables are
situated at the rear of the dining saloon. (This is known
as* badnews.*)*

Skipper's a birrovva tyrant.
*The Captain comes around once weekly to inspect the
crew's living quarters.*

Am doomee carry.
*I am doing my carry. (One of a ship's waiter's early
morning duties is to transport a barrel of beer from
the lower decks to one of the ship's many bars.)*

Seeyerrin dthe pig.
We shall meet in the Crew Bar (called, on every ship,
The Pig and Whistle*.)*

Ooze runnun dthe gamblun?
Which one of the crew is in charge of the illegal
gaming that is practised on board? (Substantial
amounts are won and lost at these games.)

Afiggot me tewthbrush.
An excuse for lateness given to the Captain each time
the ship leaves its home port. Others are:
Me wife adda kid.
Me 'ouse wuz burgled.
Me brutther died.

I yad die rear.
Dthee 'ouse wenton fire.
I yad ter goater court, juss as a witness.
(The first half of this last statement is often true.)
Then there is always the amateur psychologist who says:
Ackshully sir, I yoverslep.

Eez inniz flock . . . pist!
He is in bed, incapable. (A reply from one crew
member to a second who is inquiring as to the
whereabouts of yet a third.)

Wotsmee oaveez?
How much overtime will I be given for my working
day? (The standard question from a crew member to
the head of his department.)

*Ship's crew, especially Catering crew, work very long
hours and seven days a week. It is a very mediocre
sailor indeed who can't add an extra hour or two on
to his justly earned overtime. I do in fact know a
handsome and modest young Liverpool ex-seaman
who would book* **twelve** *hours a day* **overtime.** *Of
course he was in charge of all the overtime books.*

Isher rusband wid yer?
*A discreet inquiry from a waiter to a young married
female passenger. If the answer is in the negative, the
service for the lady immediately improves.*

Oosher cook?
Which particular chef provides your food for you?

On passenger liners all crew are supposed to eat from the crew-kitchen provided, and, while the food is often quite tolerable, it does not, naturally, compare with the passengers' menu, so a cook 'looks after you' — which means he provides any dish at all that is desired, from the passenger bill of fare. This kindness is rewarded at the end of the trip with ten, twenty, or thirty shillings, depending on how good the waiter's tips were. Hence:

Oosher cook laz?
Mirfy.
Any gud?
Grate.
Mirfy!
Wha'?
Yivgorrannudthercustimmer.

Ee gimee a dee aah!
A yelp often heard from one of the crew meaning:
The Captain stamped a D.R. in my Seaman's
Discharge Book.

D.R. indicates that the man's ability or conduct has
been so blatantly bad that the Captain 'declines to
report' on either or both. (When a wife, mother or
sweetheart is browsing through her loved one's
discharge book, sees D.R., and asks what it means,
the seaman generally mutters: Definitely Reliable.)

Ee never gibbmee me dropsy!
A declaration sometimes made by an appalled waiter
when he is given the news that one of his passengers
has died en route. (Dropsy=tip). A verbal addendum
is often:

Nossuprised ee kicked dthe buckit, used to eat like
a shitouse wrat!

It's Paahm Sundee terday.
*Means that the ship is docking on the first day of the
week and all the waiters and barmen have their hands
out for gratuities.*

*On board ship, birthdays for passengers crop up quite
frequently. The custom is for the Head Waiter to bring
in, very grandly, a birthday cake with one candle
glowing prettily on it. The waiters, generally, all crowd
round the table (anything from twenty to forty waiters,
depending on how wealthy or pretty the birthday
claimant is) and sing the time-honoured* Happy Birthday

to You. *Let me add that* **always** *a Scouse voice can be vaguely heard, an octave or two lower than the rest, singing:*

'Appy birtday tew yew, 'appy birtday tew yew,
Get plasterd yew basterd, 'appy birtday tew yew.

Story: *One particular Head Waiter — whom I'll call Mr Milner, because his name escapes me — was intensely disliked by the waiters because a) he was a would-be disciplinarian, and b) because, as one chap put it:*

Eez gorra pursnality lyka lumpa dogshit.

Nonetheless, Mr Milner had two birthdays to contend with in one night. When he brought the first cake in and asked the boys to 'sing up', they refused, as he had given them a particularly trying day, saying:

No, snorrin dthee aahrticles. *(Articles=ship's rules).*

Mr. Milner, who was rather bad on his feet, trudged gloomily to the table, set the cake down and, with a voice like a horse, sang Happy Birthday to You *completely alone, cut the cake and asked the lady to blow out the candle. He was met with a hissed:*
It's not **our** birthday, it's **theirs** on the other table!
(Whoopee!)
The second birthday was every bit as good as the first. This time Mr Milner was coming through the revolving door, cake perched precariously on his fork-like fingers, when a waiter who was literally racing in the other direction to vomit up about a quart of high velocity rum pushed the revolving door. Mr Milner, who could hardly be described as speedy, even under the best of circumstances, received a knock on the back of his

head from the swirling door, lost his balance, and
dropped the second cake. Everybody cheered.

Am entered fir dthe galley sports ternite.
As I am a kitchen worker, and because we dock in
Liverpool tomorrow, I have been assigned to cleaning
the kitchen this evening.

Aah yiz all in dthur?
Means that the second steward is checking the bell
boys' cabin to ensure that they are all in bed by nine
p.m. (regulations). One night a sixteen-year-old boy
was reported missing. After an intensive search he
was found in an engineer's cabin (the engineer was
on duty in the engine room), in bed with an eighteen-
year-old female passenger, a record player blaring, half

*a bottle of Bacardi consumed, completely at peace
with the world. He was the admiration of the entire
crew.*

Nottoo foul.
*The standard answer when one crew member asks
another:*
Ow yer doon laz?

Dthe two ringerz a birrovva snide.
The second steward or second purser is a disciplinarian.

Am doomee dhobi.
I am washing some clothes.

Fluff Alley.
The section of the ship where stenographers, stewardesses, and all other female members of the crew live.

THZE END — LIKE